T0037118

Gender Rebels

30 TRANS, NONBINARY, AND GENDER EXPANSIVE HEROES PAST AND PRESENT

KATHERINE LOCKE

ILLUSTRATED BY
SHANEE BENJAMIN

RP | TEENS
PHILADELPHIA

Copyright © 2023 by Katherine Locke
Interior and cover illustrations copyright © 2023 by Shanee Benjamin
Cover copyright © 2023 by Hachette Book Group, Inc.

Hachette Book Group supports the right to free expression and the value of copyright. The purpose of copyright is to encourage writers and artists to produce the creative works that enrich our culture.

The scanning, uploading, and distribution of this book without permission is a theft of the author's intellectual property. If you would like permission to use material from the book (other than for review purposes), please contact permissions@hbgusa.com. Thank you for your support of the author's rights.

Running Press Teens
Hachette Book Group
1290 Avenue of the Americas, New York, NY 10104
www.runningpress.com/rpkids
@runningpresskids

Printed in China

First Edition: November 2023

Published by Running Press Teens, an imprint of Perseus Books, LLC, a subsidiary of Hachette Book Group, Inc. The Running Press Teens name and logo are trademarks of the Hachette Book Group.

The Hachette Speakers Bureau provides a wide range of authors for speaking events. To find out more, go to www.hachettespeakersbureau.com or or email HachetteSpeakers@hbgusa.com.

Running Press books may be purchased in bulk for business, educational, or promotional use. For more information, please contact your local bookseller or the Hachette Book Group Special Markets Department at Special.Markets@hbgusa.com.

The publisher is not responsible for websites (or their content) that are not owned by the publisher.

Print book cover and interior design by Mary Boyer

Library of Congress Cataloging-in-Publication Data
Name: Locke, Katherine, author.
Title: Gender rebels: 30 Trans, Nonbinary, and Gender Expansive Heroes Past and Present / Katherine Locke.
Description: First edition. | Philadelphia: Running Press Teens, [2023] | Includes bibliographical references. | Audience: Ages 8–12 | Audience: Grades 4–6
Identifiers: LCCN 2022032505 | ISBN 9780762481613 (hardcover) | ISBN 9780762481620 (ebook)
Subjects: LCSH: Transgender people—History—Juvenile literature. | Transgender people—Biography—Juvenile literature. | Gender nonconforming people—History—Juvenile literature. | Gender nonconforming people—Biography—Juvenile literature.
Classification: LCC HQ77.7 .L63 2023 | DDC 306.76/809—dc23/eng/20220816
LC record available at https://lccn.loc.gov/2022032505

ISBNs: 978-0-7624-8161-3 (hardcover), 978-0-7624-8162-0 (ebook)

1010

10   9   8   7   6   5   4   3   2   1

For everyone
who lived their
truth, whether
history recorded
them or not

CONTENTS

INTRODUCTION

~~~~~~~~~~

This is a book about people. People with favorite foods, hobbies, and friends. People who like to play sports, people who like to do science, people who go to work, and people who come home to their families. People who throw balls for their pets, people who like to have grand adventures, and people who would rather stay at home.

Maybe you're someone who also has a favorite food, a hobby, and friends. Maybe you like to play sports, or do science, or both. Maybe you go to school every day and come home to your family. Maybe you have a cat or a dog you love to play with. Maybe you want to have a grand adventure, or maybe you're happy just staying home.

The point is that the people in this book are people first and foremost. They're human. They were and are complicated and messy, just like we all are. They made mistakes. They also tried and continue to try, as we all do, to live their lives as best they could and can.

For everyone in this book, however, that means living life as a different gender than the one they were assigned at birth.

Being trans, nonbinary, genderqueer, or otherwise existing outside society's expectations of gender isn't easy. No one chooses this hard path because, precisely, it's hard. They choose it because it is easier than the alternative of living a painful, confined life, squished into a box that doesn't fit or feel right.

Everyone in this book wanted and wants to live life to its fullest. They want to be happy. They want families. They want friends. They want to feel successful. They want to feel loved. And to do that, they have to live their truth as trans and nonbinary people.

This is a book about people doing their best and blazing a trail.

This is a book full of people who have experienced pain and discrimination in hopes that one day someone like them won't have to experience any pain and discrimination.

This is a book full of people just like you.

I can't wait for you to meet them.

THE SINGULAR THEY

The singular *they* has been around for hundreds of years. Geoffrey Chaucer even used it in *The Canterbury Tales*, which he wrote in 1386! *They/them* are pronouns for people who do not feel that *he/him* or *she/her* are pronouns that fit them. Pronouns can't tell you someone's gender; even so, it is very important to use them. Using the incorrect pronoun for a person is like using the incorrect name for someone. It doesn't fit, and it feels like it belongs to someone else! Being respectful of someone's pronouns is very important and helps to show that you see them as a person.

Even though *they* has been used for one person for a long time throughout human history, some people say they haven't heard of it being used this way or that they're uncomfortable using it for a singular person. The way to fix that is to use it more often! Practice, in this case, does make perfect.

Say you know someone named Jay who uses they/them pronouns. This is how you would use it in a sentence: "Jay had to take their dog on a walk. They'll be back in a minute. Oh! There they are!"

Even though the pronoun is singular, sometimes the verb is plural, as in the sentence above that says *There they are*. You wouldn't say *There they is*.

The Singular *They*

It's true that this *can* be confusing, which is why you should practice! And do you want to know a secret? You actually already know how to do this. In fact, you probably do it all the time.

Take, for example, the following sentence: "Mom, where's the delivery driver? They are late!"

In this sentence, you use the pronoun *they* for a singular delivery driver because you don't know the gender of the person who is driving the pizza to your house. And you use *they are*, not *they is*, because it's grammatically correct.

So the next time someone tells you that they don't know how to use the *they* pronoun for a singular person, you can tell them that they *do* know how and that they probably do it all the time. And it's not new! We've been using *they* for one person in English for hundreds and hundreds of years, often without realizing it.

Remember, if you have a friend who uses *they/them* and it feels a little strange to you, just practice! Soon, phrases like the ones below will be easy and effortless:

Lucy has soccer practice this afternoon. They're a goalie!

I'm going to meet Manny after school. They've got a new video game to show me. I can't wait to beat their high score!

HOW LANGUAGE, AND LABELS, EVOLVE

> **"Your name is not a song you will sing under your breath. Your pronouns haven't even been invented yet."**
>
> **–Andrea Gibson, "Your Life"**

Language is constantly changing and evolving. Can you believe that the word *internet* didn't exist a hundred years ago? And a computer used to mean a person who was doing computations rather than the machine that we have grown up with and likely have in our homes and schools. Language is always adapting as we learn more about our world, as we create more, and as we expand our ideas and definitions.

Labels, which are words and therefore part of our language, also evolve.

You'll see that some people in this book used the word *transvestite* to describe themselves. If they lived today, they might call themselves *transgender*, *drag queen*, or simply *genderqueer*, which are newer accepted

terms in our language. We don't use the word *transvestite* anymore to describe other people, but someone may still feel that it's the best word to describe *themself*. Similarly, *transsexual* is a word that is not commonly used today, but you may still see some trans individuals use it to describe themselves. You may read other words in other books that are slurs, and we no longer use them because the people who fall under those labels (but who do not use those labels personally) have asked us not to use them because they are harmful or demeaning.

Sometimes it can be confusing or frustrating to find that a word you've learned before isn't the right word to use now. That's understandable. But we should always try to keep updating our own personal dictionary as the world's dictionary expands and changes.

Did you know that being transgender used to be considered a mental disorder? Doctors called it *gender identity disorder*. People thought it was something that could be cured with therapy and psychiatric drugs. Now we know better. We know that this isn't a mental disorder and can't simply be "cured" with psychiatric drugs.

There are also pronouns you might not have heard of—*ey/em, ze/zir*—that are called *neopronouns. Neo* is a prefix that means *new*. But these pronouns have been around for a long time. *Ey/em* were coined in the 1970s, and *ze/zir* date back to 1864! Sometimes we think words, labels, and ideas are new to the world when they are really only new to us.

English-speaking people used to use the acronym LGBT—lesbian, gay, bisexual, and transgender, but now you may see LGBTQ, where the Q added at the end of the acronym stands for queer. In this book, I use LGBTQIA+ which is lesbian, gay, bisexual, transgender, intersex, and asexual along with other identities that should be included under this umbrella using the plus sign.

Some of the people in this book didn't have appropriate words or labels for their identity. They didn't know the word *transgender*. They didn't know about pronouns other than *she/her* and *he/him*, or they spoke a language that doesn't have other pronouns. Many of the people discussed in this book didn't have access to the internet, where they could have learned about words and labels that might have felt right for them. So they were forced to use the language they had available at the time where they were and with what they knew.

That's the best any of us can do—to use the language and labels we have to the best of our ability until we learn more, and then we use those words and labels. And if you are looking through this book, searching for your labels and words, and they're not here—that doesn't mean they don't exist. It just means we're still looking for them. Maybe you can be the one to discover them. I hope you share them with the world when you do, so we can keep our language and labels ever evolving to be more inclusive of who we are.

TRANS RIGHTS AROUND THE WORLD

~~~~~~~~

Trans people have been viewed differently by societies and cultures throughout history and also throughout various parts of the world. Let's take a brief look at trans rights (at the time this book was written) on every continent so you can have a better understanding of what progress has been made and what still needs to be done to spread equality to trans/nonbinary/gender expansive people globally.

NORTH AMERICA

Trans people in North America have some rights protected in each of the three countries of the continent—Canada, the United States, and Mexico. However, particularly in the United States, a recent wave of antitrans bills are being passed at the state level, endangering trans people and preventing them from safely and openly living their lives.

Still, some states score medium to high in protections for gender identity, according to the Transgender Law Center. These states are Maine, Vermont, New York, New Jersey, Massachusetts, Connecticut, Delaware, Virginia, New

Hampshire, Michigan, Illinois, Minnesota, Pennsylvania, Washington, Oregon, Nevada, California, Colorado, and New Mexico. These states have either explicitly or through court cases declared gender identity to be covered by their antidiscrimination laws.

In Canada, trans people are completely protected under national antidiscrimination laws. And in Mexico, transgender people are also covered by national antidiscrimination laws and can change their name and gender on their legal identification through a simple governmental process, which is a relatively new development.

EUROPE

Trans rights throughout Europe vary widely from country to country. Transgender individuals have some protections under European Union (EU) antidiscrimination laws, but unfortunately, they don't have full protections in the way that sexual orientation is protected under EU law.

In Europe, only Iceland and Malta recognize nonbinary identities on official documentation. And countries such as the Czech Republic, Finland, Latvia, Romania, and Slovakia have antiquated rules about medical procedures before gender changes are legally recognized. In Hungary, the current far-right regime has banned gender recognition for trans individuals.

Protections against hate speech and hate crimes against transgender people also vary widely, with the UK providing no protections against hate speech or crimes and Ireland, Denmark, and Montenegro providing the most protections for trans individuals through laws and policies.

Transgender in the EU is an organization that does annual surveys and makes policy recommendations on improving transgender rights, access to health care, protections, and related issues in the EU. Its website, tgeu.org, provides yearly updates, maps, and data.

ASIA

Asia is an extremely large and diverse continent with a wide variety of laws and rights concerning trans and nonbinary people. Most countries in Asia do not allow people to openly express a gender different than the one they were assigned at birth or to legally change their gender identity. Those countries that do allow people to change their gender identity frequently require gender affirmation surgery. (It's worth noting, however, that gender affirmation surgery should not be required to change gender identification markers on paperwork or to live as one's true gender.)

Still, there have been signs of progress in the past few years in various Asian countries. For instance, as of 2017, Vietnam recognizes transgender individuals beyond intersex (see page 5 for more on intersex). Activists and advocates have been working hard in many Asian countries to change the perception of trans and nonbinary individuals in hopes that more protections will be given to them and that acceptance of them will become commonplace.

AUSTRALIA

Transgender people are legally protected from discrimination in Australia, but whether their legal documentation can be changed and how it can be changed might depend on which state they live in. Until recently, children who wanted hormone blockers or hormone replacement therapy needed to go to court to receive a prescription and order. Now, if the child's parents and doctor all agree, a child can be prescribed hormone blockers and hormone replacement therapy without a court order in the whole country.

SOUTH AMERICA

Like other continents with a diverse population, South America has a wide variety of approaches to gender identity. Some countries are open to accepting all people and genders and have laws against discrimination; others, however, are still hostile to trans people.

But in an interesting case, the country of Argentina not only protects trans people from discrimination but also preserves 1 percent of all public sector jobs (meaning jobs in the government, from local to national) for trans people. This law was designed to help trans people get jobs in a culture and place that have a history of discrimination. This also allows trans people better access to health care and stability in a country that used to not recognize all genders.

ANTARCTICA

People don't live in Antarctica permanently, but many LGBTQIA+ scientists, including trans and nonbinary scientists, have traveled and worked there. Scientists say many of the research centers are open and friendly regarding trans rights and LGBTQ protections.

AFRICA

Africa has some of the strictest laws in the world against LGBTQIA+ people, including trans people. But progress has been made in recent years, especially in the countries of South Africa and Kenya. In Kenya—a conservative country where same-sex marriage is illegal and many parts of LGBTQIA+ life are limited—trans individuals can change their name on their official documentation, a right won in a 2014 court case. This will help trans people in that country to not be automatically outed every time they have to show their ID, including for their jobs.

In South Africa, which is the only country in Africa where same-sex marriage has been legalized and where LGBTQIA+ rights are protected in the constitution, people can change their birth gender marker in the national register and on their documentation. In recent court cases, South African courts have used the country's antidiscrimination laws to protect transgender people from discrimination and harassment.

In Botswana, a court recently ruled that gender identity markers on identification papers must be changed upon request from a trans individual. In other countries in Africa, however, it is still dangerous to be gay or transgender. LGBTQIA+ individuals in many parts of Africa risk violence, discrimination, imprisonment, and even death if they live openly.

GENDER AFFIRMATION SURGERY AND HORMONE REPLACEMENT THERAPY

Gender affirmation surgery is a surgery that helps an individual's external sex markers that often mark gender—such as breasts, vagina, penis, or testicles—match their actual gender. *Gender affirmation surgery* as a term has gone through many changes since its first use. In the past, this surgery was often referred to as a *sex change*. Today, some people call it *gender reassignment surgery*. But many prefer to use the term *gender affirmation surgery*.

For instance, a trans woman may have gender affirmation surgery that removes her penis and builds her a vagina.

It's important to know that it is *not* necessary for a trans person to undergo gender affirmation surgery if they do not want to. Surgery does not make someone more or less trans. Genitalia do not define gender. But as some trans people can be affected by gender dysphoria (see page 79 for

further information), surgery can often make a person feel more comfortable publicly presenting as their gender.

Some people choose to take hormones such as estrogen or testosterone in addition to having gender affirmation surgery, and others prefer to only take hormones to help their body's external characteristics affirm their gender. These hormones can help build or maintain certain external characteristics that help with a person's gender presentation in society.

MENTAL HEALTH AND GENDER IDENTITY

In the past, people thought being transgender was a form of mental illness. That is not true. Being transgender is not a mental illness. However, because of gender dysphoria, discrimination, trouble accessing health care, and other challenges that transgender people face, they can experience higher rates of depression, anxiety, panic disorders, and other mental illnesses as well as homelessness and unemployment.

Being transgender doesn't cause these issues. Instead, being transgender in a society or community that doesn't *support* a trans person's identity can be the cause of these issues.

The more supported a trans person is—the more welcoming and accepting their school, church, synagogue, mosque, family, community, and workplace are—the fewer mental health challenges they may experience.

Because of all the problems in the societies around us, trans people can also experience higher rates of suicide. Suicide is not the answer to any problem, however. Your voice and your story are important to this world regardless of what gender you are. Many people in this book were just like

you at your age—they didn't know how everything was going to turn out in their future. But they chose to live and to keep fighting.

If you are struggling with any issues with gender, there are resources for you (see page 90).

If you are struggling with your mental health, please reach out to the Trevor Project at www.thetrevorproject.org/get-help. It has text, chat, or phone options. It is free—24 hours a day, 7 days a week, 365 days a year. It is completely confidential.

Your story matters.

SEX WORK

~

When you look at history and trans people throughout history, you may notice sex work is a common thread.

Sex work is the occupation of providing sex or sex acts in exchange for money. And for a long time, this was one of the only professions that was open to transgender individuals, especially if they wanted to live openly as their gender instead of the gender they were assigned at birth.

Throughout history, trans people have frequently been discriminated against, so they could not get other jobs. To eat, be housed, and live, many LGBTQIA+ people turned to sex work to provide a living for themselves and even their families.

Sex work also provided trans and gender expansive people with a sense of community. Sex work, which was seen by mainstream society as lesser or immoral work, was a place where traditional gender roles were thrown out the window and where people were more welcoming, accepting, and inclusive. Additionally, sex workers have long supported each other, including creating collectives to pool resources such as housing, money, food, and protection.

Sex work continues to be a source of income, support, validation, and affirmation for LGBTQIA+ people around the globe. It's important to advocate for safe, healthy, and consensual environments for sex workers and to create communities and societies where sex work is not the only path for LGBTQIA+ people.

Sex work has historically provided a safety net for trans people worldwide, especially in places that lack acceptance and protective laws for all people. Instead of judging the people in this book who were sex workers, I encourage you to think about the circumstances that led them to sex work and what kind of support and community they found in that profession that they couldn't find elsewhere.

CALLON OF EPIDAURUS

b. approx. 250 BCE

C allon of Epidaurus was a young man who lived in the second century BCE in Greece. He was born intersex and received one of the first recorded gender affirmation surgeries in human history.

When Callon was born, he was named Callo and assigned female at birth. Back then in Greece, it was legal and normal to arrange marriages for girls when they were quite young, so Callon lived with his husband for two years before even reaching puberty. When he reached puberty, a tumor developed in his groin. Most doctors back then would not operate on him, but after some time, Callon found an apothecary— an old term for someone who practiced medicine long before medical schools existed—who agreed to do surgery to remove the tumor.

When the apothecary cut open the "tumor" on Callon's groin, he found male genitalia—testicles and a penis—tucked inside. The apothecary then performed surgery to give Callon a functional urethra through the penis, which was a dangerous and risky procedure for the second century BCE, but amazingly, in a time long before antibiotics, Callon survived.

Once he had recovered from his surgery, Callon changed his name from his birth name, Callo, to Callon and lived as a man for the rest of his life. And while we do not know much about

Callon's life in general, it does seem as if society accepted him as a man after his surgery. In fact, a record shows that he was charged with crimes for seeing women's religious ceremonies that men shouldn't see. The record of Callon's life and surgery was made by Diodorus Siculus, one of the monumental Greek historians of his time.

Callon came of age and knew his gender, which allowed him to make an informed decision about his surgery and whether he wanted to keep the genitalia discovered during the surgery or remove them. In some ways, Callon, his surgeon, and the society he lived in were more advanced and accepting of trans, nonbinary, genderqueer, and intersex individuals than some societies today.

INTERSEX

Ever wonder what the I in LGBTQIA+ stands for? It stands for intersex!

Intersex, according to InterACT, the leading intersex advocacy group in the United States, "is an umbrella term for differences in sex traits or reproductive anatomy." Intersex people either are born with these traits or develop them early (often prepuberty). For example, this can mean that their anatomy is different from their chromosomes. This happens for a variety of reasons, and there are many different combinations of these differences. In the past, people used the term *hermaphrodite*, but that is a slur, meaning a word that is violent and harmful. Even if you see it in books or media, you should not use this word. *Intersex* is the word that intersex people prefer.

Some intersex people have surgery, which they may or may not see as gender affirmation surgery, and some do not. Some people had surgery when they were little, before they could make their own decisions about what they wanted to do with their genitalia. Most intersex people advocate for people to make their own choice about whether they will receive hormone treatments or surgery.

Intersex bodies are not wrong. They are not disordered. They do not need to be fixed. Intersex characteristics are a normal part of nature and are seen in many species, not just humans. Intersexuality is just another difference in the way people's bodies look and present externally as well as internally.

CHEVALIER D'EON

1728–1810

Chevalier d'Eon was quite the character. Born in the early eighteenth century as Charles-Geneviève-Louis-Auguste-André-Timothée d'Éon de Beaumont, d'Eon lived the first forty-nine years of life as a man—fighting in wars and spying for France in both Russia and England. D'Eon was a talented spy, able to switch identities and fool nearly anyone, including infiltrating the Empress of Russia's household!

D'Eon was always subject to gender-based rumors. There was even a bet on the London Stock Exchange about it. Rumors began that she'd been born female but raised male so her father could inherit property. Some historians think that d'Eon started these rumors herself so that she could come out as a woman and live openly without anyone questioning it.

And that was exactly what she did. After a kerfuffle involving her revealing some state secrets in England, d'Eon—now forty-nine years old—returned to France and announced to the court that she was a woman and would like to live as such, using the name Charlotte-Geneviève-Louise-Augusta-Andréa-Timothéa d'Éon de Beaumont.

The court complied, in part because of the long-standing rumors, with the one requirement that d'Eon wear women's clothing if she was going to actually be a woman. (Remember, she'd been in society dressed as a man for her whole life.)

D'Eon happily complied and lived the rest of her days publicly as a woman.

When she died, doctors found that she had male genitalia, but she also had some female characteristics such as prominent breasts. It's possible that d'Eon was intersex or simply that the understanding of "female characteristics" at that time was limited and subjective.

D'Eon was a talented spy, demanding ambassador, and trans woman, all at a time when France was going through tremendous upheaval. She was truly unforgettable.

DR. JAMES BARRY

1789–1865

We don't know a lot of what James Barry thought about his own gender, and it's possible that James didn't consider himself trans. However, James referred to himself as a gentleman in all his letters, and only uses he/him in reference to himself. James was born around 1789 in Cork, Ireland, and given the name Margaret Anne. From an early age, James wanted to achieve higher education. This was difficult for girls at the time, and so, with the help of a few friends, he assumed the name James and the gender identity of a man to begin medical school in 1809, when he was eighteen years old.

Upon graduating from medical school, James joined the British Army in 1813 and quickly rose through the ranks. He implemented major changes to sanitation systems and campaigned for better living conditions for enslaved and disabled people. Wherever James saw human suffering, he sought to relieve it. He was a very good doctor, recognizing that poor sanitation, unclean water, and poor living conditions made people sick and also made it hard for them to recover. The British Army was frequently a source of these poor living conditions in the British colonies, and James worked his connections and power within the army to try to change protocols and mindsets for the betterment of all British troops.

Dr. James Barry

James lived as a man his entire adult life. When he died, his birth gender—as a female—was revealed. It caught his friends by surprise, and there was some debate later among scholars over whether James was intersex and whether that was why no one had discovered his secret. Even in letters to each other discussing James's gender, his friends remained loyal, referring to James by his pronouns and using the name he'd given them instead of the name he'd been given as a child.

WE'WHA

Approx. 1849–1896

We'wha was born into the Zuni tribe around 1849 in what is now the state of New Mexico. From an early age, We'wha expressed both male and female traits, or what the Zuni called *Ihamana*, a third-gender role in the tribe. We'wha took on many tasks normally assigned to women in the tribe, including textile art and food preparation. They were a talented weaver, with a keen eye for patterns and color combinations.

But We'wha also took on a vital role for the tribe: conservator of tribal knowledge, heritage, customs, and religion. Because We'wha was able to participate in both male and female traditions in the tribe, they had a wide and broad knowledge of tribal customs and culture.

When the US government sent anthropologists to study the Zuni, it was We'wha who shared knowledge with them and explained the tribe's customs and traditions. We'wha even traveled back to Washington, DC, as part of a delegation, where they met President Grover Cleveland. Many in Washington believed We'wha to be a cisgender woman.

Historians believe that We'wha traveled to Washington to raise awareness of the Zuni tribe in hopes that this would lead to better protection and respect for the tribe and its people. They succeeded in raising awareness, but unfortunately, the US government still committed acts of genocide against the Zuni, harming them through displacement, assimilation, and destruction of tribal customs and culture.

Nevertheless, We'wha's influence on the American public at large was important. The Zuni tribe was one of the best known of the 1880s in the United States due in large part to We'wha educating American people. And when We'wha died, they were mourned by the Zuni. With their death, the Zuni lost a leader who had a deep and broad knowledge of their customs at a time when they were under attack and being forced to assimilate; an artist who sold their work and broadened non-Zuni people's appreciation for Zuni arts; and a cultural ambassador to non-Indigenous Americans.

TWO-SPIRIT

Two-spirit is a term coined in 1990 by Myra Laramee that is used by pan-Indigenous North American people to describe a person who feels they have both a masculine and a feminine spirit inside. While European colonists in North America brought with them a strict two-gender (male-female) system, the existing diverse Indigenous communities of the continent often had a variety of gender identities and different words, terms, and ways of viewing and understanding those identities. The term *two-spirit* was invented as a way of helping First Nations/Native American people distinguish their gender identity and their culture's view of gender from the majority white/European-centric terms of the LGBTQIA+ rights movement. It's worth noting that some people may prefer more specific terms, including those specific to their tribe and/or language.

LILI ELBE

Approx. 1882–1931

*L*ili Elbe was born around 1882 in Denmark and assigned male at birth. For the first two decades of Lili's life, she lived as a man married to a fellow painter, Gerda Wegener.

When one of Gerda's models didn't show up to the studio one day, she convinced her husband to put on stockings and to dress as a woman so she could finish the painting. When Lili put on the clothing, she found herself wanting to wear those clothes more and more frequently. She started attending parties dressed as and passing as a woman. Gerda was very supportive of her husband and even suggested the name Lili— and that is what Lili went by for the rest of her life.

Back when Lili was alive and undergoing her gender affirmation surgery, medicine was not as sophisticated as it is now, and surgeons did not know enough about organ transplants. Nevertheless, Lili was one of the first people to undergo gender affirmation surgery. She had her first surgery in 1930. After she transitioned, she and Gerda divorced. Lili ended up marrying a man with whom she wanted to have children. Tragically, though, Lili's next gender affirmation surgery didn't go as smoothly, and she died of complications.

Lili's gender affirmation case opened the doors for many others who came after her. Without Lili's openness about her trans identity and her public desire for gender affirmation sur-gery, other people might have continued to feel alone and in the dark about what medical options they could pursue.

In some ways, Lili's story is tragic—her first marriage ended in divorce, and her desire to have her genitalia match the gender that she wanted to be ended in her death. But in other ways, Lili's life was full of queer love and opportunities to live as a trans woman that she might not have had in earlier eras or countries.

LUCY HICKS ANDERSON

1886–1954

When Lucy was born in 1886, her parents probably didn't know much about trans identities. Lucy was assigned male at birth but from an early age insisted that she was a girl. Her parents were worried at first and took her to a doctor who said that they should raise Lucy as a girl. So they did.

Lucy left home when she was just fifteen years old and lived as a woman. She became quite the life of the party. She was a nanny and a cook, threw church welcoming parties, and procured liquor during Prohibition for rich people's parties. She was fashionable, social, and beloved by her community. In a time when American society was highly segregated, Lucy befriended white *and* Black socialites.

Her first marriage lasted nine years before they divorced, but in 1944 she fell in love again. She married Reuben Anderson and was happily married for a year until a doctor publicly exposed her transgender identity. A court voided her marriage because the judge said that it was illegal for two men to be married and that she had lied about her gender on her marriage license.

Lucy told the court that people could be one gender but have the body of another gender, a bold proclamation for the time. "I have lived, dressed, acted just what I am, a woman," she said. "I defy any doctor in the world to prove that I am not a woman."

Lucy ended up serving jail time because the courts refused to recognize her as her husband's wife and said she'd committed fraud (a crime that comes with a jail sentence). When she was released, she and Reuben moved to San Francisco, where they lived together until her death in 1954.

Lucy was a Black trans woman in a time when it wasn't easy to be Black or a trans woman. She found happiness, fought for it, defended it, and blazed the trail for many who came after her.

BILLY TIPTON

1914–1989

Billy Tipton wanted to play jazz.

But Billy hadn't been born with the name Billy. He had been raised as a girl, and women weren't allowed to play jazz when Billy was growing up. They could sing, but they couldn't play any actual instruments. Billy, however, played both the piano and the saxophone, and he wanted to play both—on the radio! By 1933, when he was just nineteen years old, Billy started binding his breasts to disguise himself and pass as male so he could pursue his dream.

Because Billy never talked openly about his trans identity, we don't know all the details of his transition; but soon after he started to disguise himself for jazz shows, Billy began to pass as a man and lived as a man for the rest of his life.

Billy was romantically involved with many women as an adult, but he hid himself even from them. He told them that he'd been in a car accident that had disfigured him so they wouldn't ask too many questions.

Billy was an accomplished jazz musician. He founded the Billy Tipton Trio, and they eventually got a record deal. Some of their hit songs were "Can't Help Lovin' Dat Man," "Willow Weep for Me," and "What'll I Do."

Billy suffered from arthritis, however, and by the time he was in his sixties he could no longer play the music he loved the most.

No one knew Billy was trans until he died in 1989. Would he have been as successful as he was if he'd been able to live as an out-and-proud trans man? At the time when he was performing, it wasn't safe for most trans people to be out of the closet. Even though Billy kept his identity secret, his legacy shows that trans people can find joy and success in any career (and that an ear for jazz isn't limited to cisgender men).

Today, you can even find Billy's music on YouTube and other websites. Take a listen! Jazz is a conversational type of music, with instruments talking back and forth and at the same time. What might Billy have been trying to say with his music?

JIM MCHARRIS

1924–?

Born in 1924 in Mississippi, Jim McHarris knew who he was from an early age. He was raised in foster care after his parents died when he was young, and he always liked to wear men's clothing and to present himself as male, even though he'd been assigned female at birth. He transitioned in his early teens, a bold and unusual move at this time in American history.

Jim's choice to transition was brave because many places in the United States had laws against transgender people (and even if there wasn't a specific law, many local governments and law enforcement offices would find any reason to lock up trans people). Additionally, Jim was a Black man living in the South before the Civil Rights Act. At that time, Jim Crow laws (laws in the South based on race) kept Black Americans from having equal rights.

Many people in Jim's life did not know he was a trans man. His boss didn't know. His church congregation didn't know. Jim had friends and girlfriends, and he lived a happy and stable life.

After Jim was arrested for a traffic violation, the police discovered that he had been assigned a different gender at birth based on his genitalia. They accused him of impersonating a man. But Jim was not impersonating a man. He *was* a man. As he said to *Ebony* Magazine in 1954, "'I ain't done nothing wrong.'"

Sharing his story with a wider world through his interview with *Ebony* undoubtedly helped reach other Black trans men and shed light on trans issues at a time when people did not talk about topics of sex and gender identity. Jim may have lived a simple and straightforward life, but by finally being open with his trans identity in the 1950s, he blazed a trail for many to follow. There is no historical record of Jim after he moved back to Mississippi—we can only hope that he took on a new name and lived the quiet, truthful life he sought.

COCCINELLE

1931–2006

Coccinelle grew up in France during World War II, and from a young age, she knew she was a girl, even though she had been assigned male at birth. Her family was supportive of her, and she wore dresses and wigs even as a child. She even got her name from a red dress with black polka dots (*coccinelle* is the French word for ladybug).

In 1958, Coccinelle, also known as Jacqueline Charlotte Dufresnoy, was the first French trans woman to publicly receive gender affirmation surgery. Although she had been assigned male at birth, she was a woman, and so her surgery removed her penis and testicles and gave her a vagina instead. Coccinelle also legally changed her name and gender, and her first marriage was legally recognized by the French Roman Catholic Church, paving the way for transgender rights to marriage equality in France.

Coccinelle was a stage performer, and her act could be quite provocative. Her surgery helped her legally, too—until she had surgery, she could technically still have been arrested for cross-dressing, which was a crime at the time in France. Beyond her presence on the stage, Coccinelle was an activist for transgender rights. She founded Devenir Femme, which means "to become a woman," for people seeking support for gender affirmation surgery and the Center for Aid, Research, and Information for Transsexuality and Gender Identity. While neither of these organizations exists today, at the time, they were vital resources for trans people, especially trans women.

Coccinelle said that when she awoke from surgery, her surgeon said, "Bonjour, Mademoiselle," and that was how she knew it had been successful. Finally, she would be able to live the life she wanted with the body she wanted.

RENÉE RICHARDS

b. 1934

enée Richards broke barriers for trans women in professional tennis. Renée began cross-dressing in college, for which she sought therapy. She played competitive amateur tennis as a teenager and then in college and throughout her twenties while she attended medical school, graduating to become an ophthalmologist. As a competitive amateur, Renée reached the second round of the US Open men's singles in both 1955 and 1957.

When Renée transitioned in 1975, at age forty, it was a secret—until Richard Carlson (father of Tucker Carlson of Fox News) outed her on television in 1976.

Renée said she never planned to play professionally, but when she was told she couldn't, she decided she wanted to—that she *had* to. Renée told BBC News, "I told them, 'You can't tell me what I can and can't do.' I was a woman, and if I wanted to play in the US Open as a woman, I was going to do it."

To prevent her from playing professionally, the major tennis organizations required female tennis players to submit to genetic testing to prove that they were biologically female before they could compete.

Renée refused to take such genetic tests, so she was barred from playing professionally.

She then sued the United States Tennis Association (USTA) for gender discrimination. The USTA had very powerful lawyers and many witnesses who said Renée should not play against other women.

Renée's lawyer called one witness to the stand for the case. That witness was Billie Jean King—an out gay woman and professional tennis player who had won twelve Grand Slams. Billie Jean King testified that Renée's biological sex didn't give her an unfair advantage over other women. This was a great example of allyship within the LGBTQIA+ community, where one out person stood up for the rights of another.

In 1977, the judge ruled in Renée's favor. He said, "This person is now female," which sounds like a simple statement but at the time, especially in sports, was a revolutionary statement. The judge also claimed that the USTA's actions were "grossly unfair, discriminatory and inequitable, and a violation of her rights." He said the discrimination was intentional, and his judgment ultimately allowed Renée to play in the US Open.

Renée didn't win her match, but that didn't matter—she won a pivotal court case that paved the way for other trans athletes in the world of professional sports.

Despite this historic case, trans athletes continue to face discrimination to this day. While Renée's case didn't entirely end discrimination against trans athletes, it did provide a precedent for them to compete equally against athletes of their own gender, regardless of the gender they were assigned at birth.

Sports continues to be an arena in which trans people must fight for their rights and identities, but Renée Richards provides a beacon of hope that trans athletes will be able to compete at the professional level.

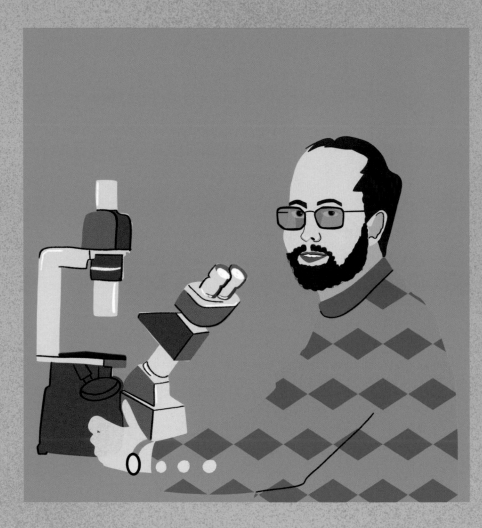

BEN BARRES

1945–2007

Ben Barres was a neuroscientist who focused all his research on glial cells, which are in the brain. Ben showed that glial cells help nerve cells develop so they can form connections for learning and memory. Glial cells also figure out which connections should stay and which can be discarded because they are not needed. Ben's research and discovery were huge developments in the field of neuroscience—made by a trans scientist.

Even more important than his research, though, was Ben's commitment to making science an equal and open playing field for all scientists. He mentored young scientists, especially LGBTQIA+ scientists. He always made time for people who were new to and curious about the field he worked in. He was also the first transgender scientist elected to the National Academy of Sciences, and he always used his platform to talk about the experiences of marginalized people in the field, including women.

Ben transitioned when he was forty-three years old, which meant he had experience as a scientist when others thought he was a woman. Since he had started his career as a woman, he was able later, as a man, to speak about the barriers women face in the scientific field.

His book *The Autobiography of a Transgender Scientist* was released after his death, but in it, he talks openly about his feelings as a young trans person before coming out and before his transition as well as his scientific study and his career. Ben's legacy of being a proud and open trans scientist paved the way for other trans scientists to come.

MARSHA P. JOHNSON

1945–1992

Marsha P. Johnson was a prominent Black trans activist, drag queen, and founder of advocacy organizations. The *P* in her name stood for "Pay It No Mind," which was what she said whenever someone wanted to question her gender.

On June 28, 1969, there was an uprising at the Stonewall Inn in New York City, a popular place for queer and trans people to gather. It was considered a safe place for people who were ostracized or in danger if they went to other bars. The police targeted the Stonewall Inn because of this and arrested many members of the queer community, including trans women, gay men, drag queens, and lesbians. The police used violence against many of the patrons of the Stonewall Inn, including in front of the growing crowd outside. This sparked riots, which continued for five more days.

The Stonewall Riots are considered the birthplace of the modern gay rights movement in the United States. It's not clear whether Marsha was there when the riots began, but she certainly joined at some point and saw this uprising as a watershed moment in the community's efforts to live peacefully without harassment from the police.

In the wake of the Stonewall Riots, gay pride parades began. And even inside the queer community there was discrimination against trans, nonbinary, and gender expansive people like Marsha. Some gay and lesbian organizers of the pride parades tried to ban Marsha and other drag queens from marching with them. But Marsha marched anyway.

When she was asked why her group was demonstrating, Marsha said, "Darling, I want my gay rights now!"

Marsha lived a colorful, big life, always looking to help other people even when she wasn't in a position to do so.

DRAG QUEEN

A drag queen is a person who uses clothing, makeup, their voice, and their mannerisms to imitate a person who uses clothing and makeup to assume female roles, usually but not always for entertainment. A drag queen may sing, dance, or otherwise perform for an audience. Drag is a way—an art—of using certain gender signifiers to subvert gender expectations. Subverting means that you expect one thing, but it's really something else. For example, a drag queen dressed in a sequined dress, with long, flowing locks and makeup but a deep masculine voice, is a way of subverting your expectations about their gender.

You might think that drag is new because of the popularity of drag-themed TV shows and events in mainstream media and culture. But drag is a very old tradition! There were drag queens (and kings) in ancient Greece and in Elizabethan England.

Drag is playful, bold, creative, and joyful. It's an art and a way of expressing gender and a way of challenging gender norms.

SYLVIA RIVERA

1951–2002

Born Ray Rivera, Sylvia Rivera was a drag queen of Puerto Rican and Venezuelan descent. She started experimenting with her clothing choices when she was a preschooler, which often got her into trouble with classmates who bullied her. Sylvia ran away from home very early in life, but luckily she met Marsha P. Johnson, who cared for her and guided her. Sylvia said Marsha was like a mother to her.

Like Marsha P. Johnson—a close friend of hers—Sylvia was at the Stonewall Riots and is sometimes credited with throwing the first brick at police. At the time, she said, "I'm not missing a minute of this—it's the revolution!" She was just seventeen years old when she helped push back against police brutality and the targeting of the queer community that gathered at the Stonewall Inn.

Her activism didn't stop there, however. Sylvia worked hard to make sure transgender people weren't excluded from the gay rights movement that sprang up out of Stonewall. And at a time when white, middle-class LGBTQIA+ people had the loudest voices in the movement, Sylvia advocated for trans people of color, especially those who lived in poverty and engaged in sex work, as she did. She faced an uphill battle within the gay rights movement, but she did not give up.

She also worked to combat homelessness among trans people—even when she was struggling with that very issue herself. She cofounded STAR—Street Transvestite Action Revolutionaries—with Marsha P. Johnson and later founded the Transy House, a transgender collective that housed trans and gender expansive people in need and served as a home base for trans activism. While neither of these organizations still exists, the Sylvia Rivera Law Project, founded in 2002, continues Sylvia's vital work of recognizing that "gender self-determination is inextricably intertwined with racial, social, and economic justice."

A street near the Stonewall Inn has been renamed Sylvia Rivera Way after this inspiring leader who was just a teenager when she said enough was enough and who paved the way for others to stand up for what is right.

RACHEL LEVINE

_____

b. 1957

Dr. Rachel Levine is the first transgender person to hold a position confirmed by the Senate. She is the assistant secretary for health for the United States (at the time this book was written) after having served as the physician general in Pennsylvania. While there are other out transgender officials throughout the ranks of government, Dr. Levine is the first one to hold an executive branch position confirmed by the US Senate.

After President Biden nominated her to the position, Dr. Levine had to go through hearings and answer questions from senators who then voted on whether they wanted her to serve in this role. They confirmed her position on March 24, 2021, making Dr. Levine the highest-ranked openly transgender person in the US government at the time that this book was written.

Dr. Levine played football as a child and attended an all-boys school. She didn't transition until she was an adult, after she'd married and had children. She says that her transition took about ten years, and she was careful with the process, both personally and professionally.

She's no stranger to hate—including some from elected US officials. But Dr. Levine says she compartmentalizes that in her mind so it doesn't get in the way of doing her job. She helped to lead the coronavirus pandemic response in Pennsylvania and then on the national stage. She also wants to tackle mental health issues and the opioid epidemic in the country. Taking care of trans youth and protecting them from bullying and other issues is part of her job as well.

After she was confirmed to her position by the Senate and sworn in, Dr. Levine told trans youth, "I have your back." And she does.

GEORGINA BEYER

b. 1957

Georgina Beyer was the first openly transgender mayor in the world and then became the world's first openly transgender member of Parliament.

While she was in high school, Georgina pursued acting and fell in love with the medium. Also as a teenager, she began to recognize her feelings about her own gender, experiencing the beginnings of gender dysphoria. But she was not able to receive gender affirmation surgery until 1984, when she was twenty-seven years old.

Three years later, Georgina's acting career led her to win a Guild of Film and Television Arts Award, the New Zealand equivalent of an Emmy in the United States.

When she was in her late thirties, Georgina became interested in politics. Her career began locally—she was elected mayor of Carterton, New Zealand, twice in the mid-1990s. From there, she ran for Parliament—and she won.

After eight years in Parliament, Georgina retired from politics. Her retirement has not kept her from being a vocal activist. But she is most proud of having been elected and having served as a member of Parliament, paving the way for trans politicians across the globe.

As someone of both European and Maori descent, Georgina has also spoken about Maori acceptance of trans individuals. According to her, the Maori used to have an inclusive attitude toward transgender people, but colonialization and Christianity upended that Indigenous inclusivity, making it difficult for trans Maori people today. Hopefully, thanks to Georgina and growing activism to recognize gender minorities in Maori communities and reclaim Maori gender identities, this will soon change.

When she was asked if she had a trans role model herself, Georgina said, "All who have given or achieved on our behalf are worthy of recognition, including those who came before us and the ones whose voices were never heard."

TAKATAAPUI

Takataapui is the Maori term for queer individuals (similar to the way *LGBTQIA+* is used as an umbrella term in the United States and other English-speaking countries). While it isn't a new term, it faded from use for a long time due to the influences of Christianity and colonialization in the Maori culture. Now people are reclaiming the term for all LGBTQIA+ identities and using it to build solidarity and activism within the community.

LANA AND LILLY WACHOWSKI

b. 1965 and 1967, respectively

Lana and Lilly Wachowski are two of the most famous filmmakers of all time—and they happen to be sisters. They are the brains behind the Matrix series, which revolutionized filmmaking in the early 2000s with its technology and storytelling.

A few years after making the Matrix movies, Lana came out as a trans woman. She was the first major Hollywood director to come out as trans. Eight years later, her sister Lilly came out as trans as well.

Both Lana and Lilly are intensely private people—they were even before they transitioned—but both have accepted several awards from LGBTQ+ advocacy organizations. One of the reasons why Lana found it important to show up and accept the award was that she didn't have trans filmmaker role models when she was a kid.

When she accepted the award, she said, "There are some things we do for ourselves, but there are some things we do for others."

Lana and Lilly have both said that the Matrix series is a trans allegory. Trans film critic Emily St. James noted that the Matrix films often address gender, showing characters choosing names that fit them better, dressing increasingly androgynously, and embracing chosen family. The films resonated with trans audiences long before Lana and Lilly came out.

Lana and Lilly have many films ahead of them, and they continue to create space in the room for trans filmmakers who've already come out, for the ones who want to come out, and for the ones who haven't even made their first film yet. It's never too late to come out, and it's never too late to start creating art.

JIN XING

---

b. 1967

Jin Xing was one of the most high-profile people in China to undergo gender affirmation surgery. After being assigned male at birth, Jin Xing grew up in China as a talented dancer and achieved special training around the world with some of the most prestigious dancers of the time. When Jin was a teenager, she both won dance competitions and enlisted in the army, where she was in a military dance troupe. She ultimately achieved the rank of colonel.

Because of her talent, she was able to study dance in New York City, which was where she began to untangle her feelings about gender and whom she was attracted to. She had not known the term *transgender* before, and once she learned it, it clicked for her.

Being transgender in China is complicated—it's not technically illegal, but it isn't common or well supported. By this point, Jin was a famous Chinese dancer, which allowed her to obtain some additional permissions from the Chinese government in getting her gender affirmation surgery.

Following surgery, she experienced some complications that almost ended her dance career. But Jin worked hard and fully recovered, returning to the stage a year later. She founded her own dance company and then participated as a judge on

China's *So You Think You Can Dance*. She became popular in China because of the show and eventually hosted her own talk show. While you may not have heard of her outside China, in her own country Jin is as famous as Oprah or Simon Cowell!

Jin doesn't feel that she's a trailblazer—she took the steps she did for herself, not as part of a larger agenda— but she still positively changed many minds in China about transgender people.

LAVERNE COX

---

b. 1972

Laverne Cox is a Black transgender woman who has used her platform as an actress to raise awareness about trans issues.

Laverne grew up in Alabama with a twin brother. From an early age, she knew she was different and was not fitting into the expected gender roles of a young boy. She loved dance and pursued it through college, where she also started pursuing an acting career.

Laverne was catapulted into the spotlight after her role on a show called *Orange Is the New Black*. She loved portraying a complex trans woman on the show, and that platform helped her break barriers both in TV and in society. Furthermore, in a positive leap forward for trans actors, Laverne has *also* played cis female characters on TV. In this way, she has set the example that trans women *are* women and can be cast as such, regardless of whether the character is cis or trans.

Laverne was the first trans person to be nominated for a prime-time Emmy, the first trans person on the cover of *Time* magazine, the first trans person on the cover of *Cosmopolitan*, and the first trans person with a wax model at Madame Tussauds (a famous museum in London that creates wax figures of famous people).

Laverne has used her platform to advocate for trans and gay rights, to lift up other trans people, and to bring awareness to the trans community. She has won many awards for her trans advocacy work as well.

One of her goals is to increase the visibility of trans people without a focus on the actual *transition* between genders. As she says, "It is revolutionary for any trans person to choose to be seen and visible in a world that tells us we should not exist."

ERIN PARISI

b. approx. 1977

Erin Parisi is climbing to new heights.

Literally.

Erin, the founder of TranSending—an organization that uses athletics to champion trans inclusion—is the first out trans climber to summit Vinson Massif, the tallest peak in Antarctica (sixteen thousand feet tall), where it reaches -52 degrees Fahrenheit at the peak. She planted a trans pride flag at the top once she reached it. Vinson Massif is the fifth major mountain Erin has summited, and she has her eyes on two more: Mount Everest and Denali. She'll take her trans pride flags up those mountains, too.

Erin is committed to raising the profile of trans athletes and to promoting trans rights in sports. She's a lifelong athlete and believes children should be able to play sports on the teams that align with their gender.

When Erin came out in 2016, she wasn't sure she'd be able to continue climbing. She hadn't read about any trans climbers. Most of the news stories she read about trans people involved violence or discrimination. But she kept climbing despite all of that, and now she wants to share the uplifting news that being trans doesn't mean you have to give up the things you love. Now she can climb *and* live her life proudly and authentically.

The current big challenge that she's taking on is the Seven Summits. This is a notorious challenge for climbers who aim to climb the highest peak on every continent. The seven big mountains were all first summited in 1985 and have been completed by fewer than five hundred people since then—and never by an out trans person.

Erin wants to be the first, but she doesn't want to be the last.

AMARANTA GÓMEZ REGALADO

b. 1977

Amaranta Gómez Regalado, who uses both *she/her* and *they/them* pronouns, loves books. In fact, they picked their name when they were a teenager from a book, *A Hundred Years of Solitude*, by Gabriel García Márquez. As the character in the book struggles in life, Amaranta Gómez Regalado has worked hard to ensure that they, and other muxhe people, live fulfilling, happy lives.

Amaranta is an Indigenous person living in Oaxaca, Mexico, and belongs to the Zapotec Indigenous community. *Muxhe* is a term unique to the Zapotec people. Muxhe are always assigned male at birth, but they are not male. Their identity is about who they are, not whom they're attracted to. Muxhe can be gay, straight, bisexual, pansexual, or asexual. The term *muxhe* is about a person's gender identity, which some say is a third gender and others say is more complicated than that. This idea is reflected in their language, too. Unlike Spanish, the Zapotec language is entirely gender neutral. The culture accepts and provides language for more than two genders in ways that many languages and cultures do not.

When Amaranta was a teenager, they chose their new name and began a life of advocacy. When they were just twenty-five years old, they founded their own political party: México Posible. They were the first transgender person to run for office in all of Mexico. While they didn't win the election, they did break down barriers and brought the language and identity of the muxhe to a larger stage. Today, they continue to be an advocate for HIV prevention and speak out against homophobia and discrimination against the muxhe.

Zapotec culture shows us that there are many cultures without binary gender systems. There are many things to learn from a culture that has protected and created space for people to discover who they are and to feel supported along the way.

GENDER NEUTRAL

Gender neutral means that something was created without a specific gender in mind. You may hear someone say that a name is gender neutral. For example, the name *Alex* can be used for any gender, and people do not automatically think of a certain gender when they hear it. Yellow is often used as a gender-neutral color for baby clothes, while blue and pink have been highly gendered in society. Gender neutral isn't always the most inclusive state, though. Instead of calling a bathroom *gender neutral*, the better term would be *all-gender bathroom*. That way, instead of saying, "This wasn't made for a specific gender," society would be saying, "This was made for all genders." That is the power of inclusivity.

LAXMI NARAYAN TRIPATHI

---

b. 1978

When Laxmi was born in India in 1978, a parent could choose only one of two genders for their child on official paperwork: male or female. However, India actually has a long history of accepting gender minorities. *Hijra* is the word for asexual, intersex, or transgender people in India, and people identifying as hijra have had their own communities, ways of practicing the Hindu religion, traditions, and support systems for a very long time.

It was the British colonial system that brought in the idea of a gender binary to India, and the British government enacted laws against people who did not fit neatly into the "male" or "female" box. Even after the British colonial system ended, the trauma and prejudice of this era endured, affecting all the hijra.

Laxmi was determined to change this. As soon as she connected with the hijra community, Laxmi became an activist, fighting for change and for recognition of the rights of gender minorities in India and around the world. She organized protests, gave a speech at the UN in 2008, and led the charge for three gender choices to be on all official documents. And in 2014, she and all the trans and intersex people of India won their case. The law was also changed to allow hijra people in India to adopt children and to change their gender on their paperwork after gender affirmation surgery.

Laxmi has been a proud change maker in India for more than two decades now, helping to undo the painful colonial legacy that the British left behind and to bring back the traditional value and importance of hijra to Indian culture.

HIJRA

Hijra is an umbrella term on the Indian subcontinent (which contains India, Bangladesh, Bhutan, the Republic of Maldives, Nepal, Pakistan, and Sri Lanka) for intersex, asexual, or transgender people. That covers a lot of ground! Hijra is a recognized third gender on the continent, dating back centuries in both mythology and the historical record. While colonialization targeted hijra, efforts have been made to reclaim the term and identity in these countries. In many, it can even be a gender identifier on passports. Even though *hijra* is used on most of the continent, it's important to know that this word can be seen as a slur in Urdu, the primary language of Pakistan, where the term *Khawaja Sara* is used instead.

LAUREL HUBBARD

b. 1978

New Zealander Laurel Hubbard is the first openly transgender woman to compete in the Olympic Games.

Laurel was assigned male at birth and raised as a boy. She competed in weight lifting as a junior in high school but stopped competing a few years later. She transitioned in 2012, at the age of thirty-five, and started weight lifting again shortly after that.

It didn't take her long to climb the ranks of competitive weight lifting. She won silver at the 2017 World Championships and gold at the Oceania Championships in 2019.

In 2015, the International Olympic Committee allowed trans women to compete as women at the Olympic Games. Five years later, in 2020, Laurel was the first trans woman to qualify for the Olympics under this ruling.

This was controversial for many people, however. Some antitrans advocates said that Laurel's chromosomes meant she had an unfair advantage over other women in the competition.

Laurel did not let any of that bother her. She did what she's done since she transitioned and kept weight lifting. She kept her head down and kept her focus. While she didn't win an Olympic medal, Laurel went out there and did her best, thanking all her supporters along the way.

It is not easy to be a trailblazer, especially on a big stage like the Olympics. But Laurel carried that responsibility with ease. She earned a gold medal in poise, focus, and blazing a trail for the trans women athletes who will come after her.

AUDREY MBUGUA

b. 1984

Audrey Mbugua is a transgender activist in Kenya, where strong gender norms and societal discrimination pose many challenges. Transgender individuals are often victims of violence in Kenya, and they are also often refused jobs and health care access.

In fact, Audrey's family cut her off when she came out as trans. The suicide rate among transgender people in Kenya is very high. Audrey did not want to become a statistic.

Audrey could not find a job while her name and gender didn't match what was on her academic transcripts and diploma. She was often accused of stealing someone else's identity, but that wasn't true.

So Audrey took the issue to court in a highly publicized way. It can be scary and dangerous to go public in this way, especially in Kenya, but Audrey knew that she was fighting not just for herself in that courtroom but for all trans people in her country.

The courts finally ruled in Audrey's favor, and her paperwork was changed to match her identity as a woman. Additionally, Audrey even won a second legal case. When she first founded her nonprofit organization called Transgender Education and Advocacy, the government refused to list it as an approved nongovernmental organization. But the courts also found that this was discrimination and that there was no legal basis for it.

By using the courts to recognize her rights, Audrey paved the way for other transgender people in Kenya. She's a trail-blazer, and she has not stopped fighting for a society that supports transgender people without discrimination.

JANELLE MONÁE

b. 1985

Janelle Monáe doesn't like to be boxed in to one thing (who does, really?). She's a musician, an actress, and an author—and who knows what she'll do next?

When she was young, Janelle moved to New York City to attend the American Musical and Dramatic Academy. She was the only Black woman in her class there. She said it felt like a home, but she always worried that she might lose what made her Janelle. If she started thinking, acting, singing, and performing like everyone else, she'd lose what made her feel most like herself—and what got her noticed in the first place.

So Janelle made it a goal to always be herself and to never take the easy path of blending in with the crowd.

She started her career as a rapper and a musician. Her diverse music pulls from a variety of traditions, including blues, jazz, soul, and pop. She's influenced by Stevie Wonder and Prince, an artist who was also known for gender creativity.

She has also starred in historical films, such as *Harriet* and *Hidden Figures*, and has written science fiction short stories based on her album *Dirty Computer*.

Janelle approaches her gender the same way that she approaches her work. After she contributed to a hashtag trend, #IAmNonBinary, Janelle said in an interview, "I feel my feminine, I feel my masculine, I feel energy that I can't really explain." She came out officially on Jada Pinkett Smith's show, *Red Table Talk*, in April 2022, saying, "I'm nonbinary, so I don't just see myself as a woman, solely."

Janelle could have decided to let herself be boxed in and labeled, especially in an industry like Hollywood, where sure bets are safer and experimentation is often criticized. But Janelle wants to live a genuine life that allows her to feel true to herself. Just as she pushes boundaries and lives outside conventions in her art, she also pushes these boundaries when it comes to her gender and sexuality.

ELLIOT PAGE

b. 1987

Elliot Page had already made a name for himself as an actor by winning awards as Ellen Page when he came out as trans. He shared his new name and his new pronouns with the world in a brave and vulnerable Instagram post that touched the hearts of millions worldwide.

When Elliot was young, he wanted to grow up to be a boy. He imagined himself as a boy, even as the world continued to perceive him as a girl. When he came out as gay, he was able to start wearing more masculine clothing and choosing roles that felt more suited to him—but it still wasn't enough. Anxiety and depression were a part of Elliot's life, stemming in part from his struggle with gender dysphoria.

Inspired by other trans celebrities and by trans writers, Elliot finally decided to be the person he was. He began by changing his name and then his pronouns, and finally he got gender affirmation surgery. As he stepped more fully into himself, Elliot found that the world was more bearable, less anxiety producing, and less depressing.

He also knew that he was transitioning from a place of privilege and that part of his responsibility was to raise awareness of the antitrans legislation sweeping the United States. He used his coming-out letter on Instagram to celebrate the trans people who came before him and to draw awareness to the trans people suffering under bigotry and oppression in the world today.

The continued growth of Elliot's Hollywood career shines a light for young trans actors who want to make acting a profession, whether they star in independent films or big superhero franchises. And Elliot's advocacy will hopefully help turn the tide against transphobia in this crucial time.

GENDER DYSPHORIA

Gender dysphoria is the feeling a person has that they are a different gender than the one they were assigned at birth based on their genitalia. These feelings can be very intense and strong and can frequently be a source of anxiety, depression, and stress. Think of gender dysphoria as the distance between the gender you were assigned and the gender you feel yourself to be. The bigger that distance is, the more stress, anxiety, depression, and other mental health symptoms you may experience. The shorter the distance, the less stress this will likely have on your mind and body. Addressing gender dysphoria is all about bringing the gender you are seen as closer to the gender you know you are. This may mean dressing differently, using a different name and/or pronouns, hormone replacement therapy, gender affirmation surgery, or all of the above.

TOMOYA HOSODA

---

b. 1991

omoya Hosoda was not the first trans person elected to public office in Japan (that was Aya Kamikawa), but he is the first out trans man and one of the only out trans men in public office in the world.

Tomoya was elected to the Iruma City Council in 2018, and his continued hope is that his higher-profile position will help raise awareness of gender and transgender issues in his country. In Japan, access to hormone replacement treatment and gender affirmation surgery requires being diagnosed with a mental illness—what is labeled a gender identity disorder. This used to be the case in the United States, too, and isn't uncommon in other countries around the world. But it does mean that there's a significant barrier to accessing services for trans people.

Tomoya wants to break down that barrier.

When Tomoya was a young trans man—before he transitioned—he did not think he could be happy. But after meeting a trans man online who supported and encouraged him, Tomoya came out to his parents. He took that courageous step with his family, recognizing that coming out is just the beginning. His path was made smoother by Aya Kamikawa, who advocated for a change in Japanese law to allow trans people to change their gender on their official documents.

The law was passed in 2005, when Tomoya was only fourteen years old.

Though much of his work on the City Council is general planning, such as updating traffic lights and reviewing budgets, Tomoya hopes that he can also help change minds and raise awareness of trans individuals in Japan due to his elevated position. It takes trailblazers like Tomoya to show that trans people can be successful in a number of careers, whether locally or worldwide.

TALLEEN ABU HANNA

b. approx. 1995

When Talleen, an Arab Christian Israeli, was growing up, she always wanted to wear dresses and look cute. But the older she got, the more demanding gender norms—in her case, acting like a boy—became. She didn't have the language to know what her feelings were until she went to a party as a teenager where she met a trans woman. Talleen said she held on to that knowledge like a rope that was going to save her—the understanding that she wasn't alone in her feelings and that there were other people like her in her community.

Talleen transitioned in 2015, and a year later she competed in Miss Trans Israel, winning the competition and earning a spot in an international beauty pageant in Barcelona. She has also been on the Israeli version of the reality TV show *Big Brother*. She now works as a dancer, an actor, and a model.

Talleen has had to overcome prejudice in her community, as well as in her family, due to her transition. While her mother supported her, her father was initially upset by her coming out, and they did not speak for years until they finally reconciled. Talleen said much of her father's concern came from shame within the community, and she hopes one day to help counsel other Arab Christians who wish to come out as transgender to break through that perceived shame and to allow better acceptance of trans people within families as well as the community.

JAZZ JENNINGS

b. 2000

Jazz Jennings is one of the youngest people to go public with her transgender identity. Jazz started to express a desire to be a girl when she was just two years old, and her family supported her desire to present as a girl and eventually helped her to medically transition as she grew older.

Jazz wrote a picture book called *I Am Jazz* to educate young people about her story. She and her family also starred in a reality TV show with the same name. The show, which allowed the Jennings family to talk openly about transgender identity and the challenges trans people must face, was very influential in helping trans kids and their families feel less alone. It also provided families and kids who are cisgender with the language to talk respectfully about and to transgender people.

Jazz has been an extraordinary spokeswoman for trans people in the United States, and her show helped people see that as a trans kid, she was incredibly happy. She wasn't disturbed or abused or mentally ill. She was simply a normal kid growing up as the gender she knew herself to be. That made a huge difference for thousands of trans kids and their parents.

One of the main reasons Jazz has been so public with her journey as a trans woman is that she wants other trans kids to know they aren't alone, at any age, and that embracing who they are is not always easy, but it's ultimately the path to hopefully finding happiness and fulfilment in life.

GLOSSARY

BINARY: A term for when there are two of something, like on or off. In this book, we talk about the gender binary, or the false idea that there are only two genders (male and female). People in this book break the binary by showing that there are many ways to experience and to express gender.

CIS: A term you may see with the words *gender*, *person*, *people*, *woman*, or *man*. This means that the gender assigned to a person at birth based on their physical sex characteristics aligns with the gender they feel internally.

DISCRIMINATION: This means unfair or biased treatment, usually under a law. For instance, if someone is fired from a job solely because they are trans, that would be discrimination because it is unfair treatment (because cis people don't get fired for being cis, for example).

GENDER: Sometimes people use the terms *gender* and *sex* interchangeably, but gender is *identity* and is not tied to any physical traits. It's about our internal experience of who we are and our ability to name that experience. Gender is a spectrum with many variations, not a binary. People live and experience gender in many ways, including within a gender. There is not one way to be a woman or a man, and there isn't one way to be nonbinary, trans, or genderqueer, either.

GENDER AFFIRMATION SURGERY: A term for a surgery that helps people align their physical sex characteristics with their gender.

GENDER DYSPHORIA: A phrase for when someone experiences mental, physical, emotional, and/or psychological distress from not living and expressing themself as their true gender.

GENDER EUPHORIA: A phrase for the elation, joy, happiness, and "rightness" that come from living and expressing oneself as one's true gender.

GENDER EXPRESSION: This is how someone's body language, voice, clothing, mannerisms, interests, etc. all come together to express their gender outwardly to others.

GENITALIA: A term for physical sex characteristics and organs, such as testicles or vaginas.

LGBTQIA+: An acronym that stands for lesbian, gay, bisexual, transgender, queer (or questioning), intersex, asexual, and more. It is used as an umbrella term for the entire community. You may see this shortened sometimes as LGBTQ or LGBT+.

PRONOUN: A word that replaces a noun. For instance, *he* is a pronoun. In the sentence "Thomas loves to ride his bike," you could replace *Thomas*, a proper noun, with *he*, a pronoun.

TRANS: This word can be used as an adjective to describe things relating to transgender people or to transgender identity. For instance, trans rights are civil rights relating to transgender people, and trans advocacy is advocacy of transgender people.

TRANSGENDER: A term that means someone who was assigned one gender at birth (usually based on physical sex characteristics such as genitalia) but who is actually a different gender. For instance, a woman who was assigned male at birth based on the presence of a penis is a trans woman. Some nonbinary, genderqueer, gender expansive, and intersex people also identify as trans. Some prefer to remain distinct. This is up to the individual.

TRANSITION: This can be used as a noun or a verb to describe a trans person's change from living as one gender to living as another. It can be as simple as a name change or as complicated as gender affirmation surgery.

RESOURCES

GENDER SPECTRUM is an organization that seeks to create gender-friendly and open, welcoming spaces for children and teens. There are resources for parents and teachers as well. https://genderspectrum.org/

THE MARSHA P. JOHNSON INSTITUTE supports and advocates for Black trans people. https://marshap.org/

TRANS LIFELINE is an organization devoted to helping trans people get the support and access to care they need when they need it. https://translifeline.org

TRANSENDING is an organization devoted to supporting trans rights in athletics. https://www.transending7.org/

TRANSGENDER IN THE EU tracks updates to trans rights and policies throughout the European Union. https://tgeu.org

TRANSGENDER LAW CENTER is a community-led action organization advocating for trans rights and inclusion. https://transgenderlawcenter.org/

THE TREVOR PROJECT is an organization specifically for LGBTQIA+ young people who need resources, advice, support, and hotlines when they are in crisis. There are text options as well. https://www.thetrevorproject.org

ACKNOWLEDGMENTS

Thank you to my whole family, who have always loved me for
who I am—messy, complicated, covered in cat hair, perpetually late,
nonbinary, loud, bossy, sensitive, and silly. I love you all so much.

I'm grateful to my friends, and especially all my trans and
nonbinary friends who embraced me and gave me a home
and support when I needed it the most.

Thank you to my wonderful agent, Lara, for all her support,
guidance, advice, and cheerleading from the sidelines.

And thank you to Julie Matysik and Val Howlett for bringing me to this
project, for your kindness and empathy, for your curiosity and support, and for
your vision and bravery. It isn't easy sending a book like this into the world, and
I'm so glad that all the *Gender Rebels* and I have you on our side.

Thank you to designers Frances J. Soo Ping Chow and Mary Boyer,
illustrator Shanee Benjamin, production editor Sean Moreau, copy editor
Connie L. Oehring, and proofreaders Susie Pitzen and Emily Epstein White
for your expertise. Thank you to Betsy Hulsebosch and Becca Matheson
for your support and enthusiasm!

And thank you for every librarian, teacher, and parent who puts
this book in classrooms, libraries, and the hands of readers.

And thanks to you, trans and nonbinary readers, for being brave.
Thank you for living your truth, however you can, every day.
You matter. I am so glad you're in this world.